All kinds of Dolls

James Dunbar

OXFORD
UNIVERSITY PRESS

UNIVERSITY PRESS

Great Clarendon Street, Oxford, OX2 6DP

Oxford University Press is a department of the University of Oxford.
It furthers the University's objective of excellence in research, scholarship,
and education by publishing worldwide in

Oxford New York

Athens Auckland Bangkok Bogotá Buenos Aires Calcutta
Cape Town Chennai Dar es Salaam Delhi Florence Hong Kong Istanbul
Karachi Kuala Lumpur Madrid Melbourne Mexico City Mumbai
Nairobi Paris São Paulo Singapore Taipei Tokyo Toronto Warsaw
and associated companies in Berlin Ibadan

Oxford is a registered trade mark of Oxford University Press
in the UK and in certain other countries

A CIP record for this book is available from the British Library

ISBN 0 19 915590 9
Available in packs
Toys Pack of Six   (one of each book)   ISBN 0 19 915595 X
Toys Class Pack   (six of each book)   ISBN 0 19 915617 4

Printed in Hong Kong

Acknowledgements

The Publisher would like to thank the Victoria and Albert Museum
(pp 3 *bottom right*, 6 *bottom right*, 10 *left*) for permission to
reproduce photographs.

All other photography by Martin Sookias.

With special thanks to Marianne Caunter, Mo Chandler,
Emily Clements, James Dunbar, Jane Harley, Tim Porter,
George Taylor, Mavis Thomson, Geoff Tombs, and Sarah Wallis
for the loan of dolls.

Introduction

Dolls are made from many different materials. This reference book will tell you about some of them.

Contents

 Fabric dolls 6

 Wooden dolls 8

 China dolls 10

 Metal dolls 11

 Plastic dolls 12

Different sorts of dolls 14

Paper dolls 14

Bead dolls 14

Bendy dolls 15

Puppets 15

Index 16

Fabric dolls

Some dolls are made of fabric like wool, cotton, and nylon. Some fabric dolls are soft and cuddly.

This scarecrow is made of wool.

This rag doll is made from pieces of fabric. It is filled with fabric to make it soft.

Fabric dolls can also be quite firm and hard.

This doll is made of fabric. It is decorated with beads and metal bangles. It is from South Africa.

This doll is from Namibia in Africa. She is wearing a traditional costume.

7

Wooden dolls

Wooden dolls feel strong and hard. The wood is cut into different shapes. Wooden dolls are often painted.

This Dutch doll is wooden. Her legs and arms move. ▶

These Russian dolls fit inside each other. They are all painted differently. ▼

This wooden doll is from Germany.

These dolls are from Egypt.

This doll's head is wooden but its body is made of fabric.

China dolls

Long ago, children played with dolls made of china. The children had to be very careful because china breaks easily.

These china dolls are over 100 years old.

This is a modern china doll. Some people collect dolls like this.

Metal dolls

Some dolls are made of metal. Metal can be bent into different shapes, and it does not break easily.

You push this metal toy along the ground.

This toy is made of tinplate. It is over 60 years old.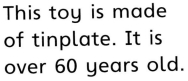

This soldier is over 70 years old. It is made of a metal called lead.

Plastic dolls

Many dolls are made of plastic.
Plastic is smooth and strong,
and it can bend.

This plastic baby
doll looks like a
real baby.

This doll's head, arms,
and legs move. It is
over 50 years old.

These dolls are dressed to show where they come from.

These dolls are wearing Japanese costume.

This plastic doll is wearing Maori costume. She is from New Zealand.

Different sorts of dolls

Dolls are made from all sorts of materials. Here are a few more.

This doll is made of paper. You can change its clothes.

These dolls are made of beads and wire.

These dolls have metal wire inside them, so you can bend their legs and arms.

This wooden doll is a puppet. If you move the sticks his arms move.

Index

Africa   7

china   10

cotton   6

Dutch   8

Egypt   9

fabric   6–7, 9

firm   7

Germany   9

hard   7, 8

Japanese   13

lead   11

metal   7, 11, 15

New Zealand   13

nylon   6

plastic   12

Russian   8

smooth   12

soft   6

strong   8, 12

tin   11

wooden   8–9, 15

wool   6